PEBBLES IN MY POCKET

A Collection of Motivational Affirmations

By

KELVIN HARRIS

PEBBLES IN MY POCKET

First Edition

ISBN Paperback: 979-8-9940553-0-4
ISBN Hardcover: 979-8-9940553-1-1
ISBN eBook: 979-8-9940553-2-8

TABLE OF CONTENTS

“Be here now. Begin where your feet touch earth.”

K.H

CHAPTER 1

Begin Where You Stand

"Wherever you are, be all there!"

JIM ELLIOT

You're not stuck. You're stalling. And there's a difference.

Stuck means the tires don't move. Stalling means the car is running, but you're still sitting in the driveway waiting for divine Wi-Fi to download your destiny. Spoiler: it won't.

Here's the hard truth: tomorrow is just a rumor. The only RSVP you can make is today.

Harvard psychologist Daniel Gilbert discovered that humans are terrible at predicting what will make us happy. 1 We obsess about the future as if it's guaranteed, but science says otherwise. We overplan. We overthink. We under-live.

Our real life happens in the present tense—and you're missing the party. Presence isn't just spiritual fluff. Yale researchers found that people who trained in present-moment awareness had significantly lower stress and higher well-being.[2] Translation? Your brain rewards you for showing up in the now.

---

[1] Matthew A. Killingsworth and Daniel T. Gilbert, "A Wandering Mind Is an Unhappy Mind," *Science* 330, no. 6006 (2010): 932, https://doi.org/10.1126/science.1192439.

[2] Ibid.

"Today is always here.
Tomorrow? A whisper."

K.H.

So, why are you still waiting for Monday? For the promotion? For the perfect sign? Here's a secret: the sign is the fact that you're breathing. That's it. No thunderbolt required.

Here's what waiting really does: it turns you into a collector of excuses. And excuses are like rocks in your pocket—heavy, distracting, and they slow you down. The more you carry, the harder it is to move.

Start where you are, with what you have, even if it feels small. *Especially* if it feels small. Because small starts compound into unstoppable momentum. Every bestselling book began with a messy draft.

Presence is powerful because it doesn't negotiate. It doesn't ask you to be perfect. It just asks you to show up.

And showing up is the gateway to everything else.

Neuroscience backs this up, too. Stanford researchers found that when people engage fully in a task (no distractions, no multitasking), their brains light up in areas tied to satisfaction and mastery. Focus creates fulfillment. Multitasking, by contrast, scatters energy like confetti in a hurricane—seconds of satisfaction, useless after.

So plant your feet. Look around. Take the first step. The ground you're on is already enough. Regret weighs more than failure. And here's the deal: failure is recyclable. Regret is not. You can use failure as compost for your growth. Regret just rots.

The invitation of presence is this: to live now, so your future self thanks you instead of resents you.

Start now. Begin where you stand. Even if it's messy. Even if it's scary. Even if you're not ready. Because *ready* is a myth. *Courage* is action in the face of *not-ready*.

And that first step you've been avoiding? That's the pebble that starts the ripple.

"I begin where I stand."

K.H.

"Today is always here. Tomorrow? A whisper."

K.H.

CHAPTER 2

The Whisper of Tomorrow

"The future depends on what you do today."

MAHATMA GANDHI

Tomorrow is seductive. It's shiny, it's hopeful, it's full of promises. But tomorrow doesn't exist yet. It's an excuse your brain makes to avoid action today.

When you say, "I'll start tomorrow," what you're really saying is, "I'm scared today." Fear disguised as planning is still fear.

Research in psychology calls this "temporal discounting." We value future rewards more than present effort. It feels easier to push the work onto your future self because you imagine they'll be more disciplined, more confident, more prepared. Spoiler: they won't. They'll still be you.

Harvard studies on procrastination reveal that our brains are wired to avoid discomfort in the short term, even if it sabotages us in the long run. That's why we scroll instead of start, plan instead of execute, dream instead of do.

Yale researchers studying stress patterns found that anticipation of a task is often more stressful than the task itself. Translation:

the idea of action tomorrow creates more anxiety than actually doing it today.

So when you delay, you're not avoiding pain—you're multiplying it.

Let's be honest, *tomorrow* is just a polite word for *never*. Because if it mattered, you'd start now.

Think about it. Every invention, every success, every revolution—none of them happened *tomorrow*. They all happened in the only place they could: today.

Tomorrow is tempting because it lets you off the hook. It tells you the lie that you'll be stronger later. But strength is built now. Confidence is built now. Momentum is built now.

Stop outsourcing your life to a version of you that doesn't even exist yet. Your future self is waiting for you to stop stalling and start moving *today*.

Tomorrow is a whisper. Today is a shout. And life only answers the loud.

Take one step now, even if it's small, even if it's messy. Because messy action today beats perfect plans tomorrow.

"I act today.
Tomorrow is too quiet."

K.H.

"Every day is a question from God. Let the silence answer."

K.H.

CHAPTER 3

Silence Is the Answer

"The quieter you become, the more you can hear."

RAM DASS[3]

Silence has a bad reputation. We treat it like an awkward pause, something to fill with chatter, noise, or the endless scroll of distraction. But silence is not empty.

Silence is full of answers, clarity, and the truths that only arrive when the world gets quiet enough for you to hear them.

Modern psychology agrees. Research from Harvard Medical School shows that intentional silence—whether through mindfulness, prayer, or meditation—actually rewires the brain. It increases gray matter in areas associated with learning, memory, and emotional regulation. Translation: silence makes you smarter, calmer, and more resilient.

Yale researchers have studied how chronic noise raises cortisol, spikes heart rate, and weakens the immune system. Noise isn't just annoying; it's toxic. Silence is the antidote.

---

[3] Ram Dass, *Be Here Now* (San Cristobal, NM: Lama Foundation, 1971).

"Listening is love. Let your ears open your heart."

K.H.

But silence isn't passive. It's powerful. It's the pause before the breakthrough, the breath before the answer, the stillness where action is born.

And when you linger in silence, you hear life questions: Who are you becoming? What matters now? What do you need to let go of?

The truth is, most people are terrified of silence. Because it tells the truth. It reveals what busyness tries to hide. But if you're brave enough to sit in it, you'll discover the voice you've been drowning out—your own.

So the next time life feels noisy, don't reach for distraction. Reach for silence. Because silence isn't absence—it's presence, magnified.

Every day is a question from God. Let the silence answer.

"In silence, I hear the truth."

K.H.

"Denial doesn't destroy reality. But truth will always bloom through cracks."

K.H.

CHAPTER 4

Cracks of Truth

"The truth will set you free."

JOHN 8:32

Truth is a stubborn guest. You can ignore it, deny it, or try to cover it with excuses, but eventually it kicks down the door and sits at your table anyway.

Denial is seductive. It whispers, "If I don't look at it, it's not real." But denial doesn't destroy reality. It delays your freedom. Because truth always blooms, even through the cracks you tried to seal shut.

Psychologists call this "cognitive dissonance"—the mental stress that comes from holding two conflicting beliefs. Say you want to live healthily, but you keep numbing yourself with fast food. Or you crave love, but you sabotage it because you don't feel worthy. The gap between what you want and what you live creates inner chaos.

Yale researchers found that when people live in denial, their stress markers spike. Heart rate increases, cortisol rises, and decision-making plummets. Your body knows the truth even when your mind refuses to admit it.

So what happens when you stop running? You face reality—and while it may sting, it heals faster than the lies.

"Chew carefully. Not all sweetness is truth."

K.H.

The greatest transformations in history weren't built on denial. They were built on truth. Civil rights, scientific breakthroughs, revolutions—they all started when someone dared to face reality head-on.

Personal growth works the same way. You can't heal what you won't name. You can't fix what you won't face. You can't free yourself while you're still in denial.

So here's your invitation to drop the sugar coating. Embrace the sting. Because truth may hurt for a moment, but lies will starve you forever.

"I choose truth, even when it stings."

K.H.

"To love is a tall order. Stand anyway."

K.H.

CHAPTER 5

Stand Anyway

"Courage is grace under pressure."

ERNEST HEMINGWAY

Love and courage are twins. You can't have one without the other.

To love deeply is to risk deeply. It means exposing your heart to rejection, failure, and disappointment. It means standing tall when every voice—including your own—tells you to shrink back.

But fear doesn't mean you're weak. Fear means you're on the edge of something meaningful.

Harvard Business Review published studies showing that courage is not the absence of fear, but action in the presence of it. Firefighters, soldiers, entrepreneurs—they all admitted to fear. The difference was, they stood anyway.

Yale research on vulnerability shows that humans bond more deeply when we risk emotional honesty. When you open yourself to love—even when it's scary—you create connections that denial never could. Courage isn't about avoiding the fall. It's about standing despite knowing the fall may come.

You don't wait for guarantees. You don't wait until rejection is impossible, or risk is erased. Because waiting for certainty is waiting forever.

Think about every great act of love, service, or leadership—it wasn't done by the fearless. It was done by the fearful who stood anyway.

So what does this mean for you? It means stop waiting until you feel ready. Stop waiting until you've got every safety net in place. *Ready* is a myth. Courage requires risk.

To love is a tall order. But to stand anyway is to live tall.

And when you stand tall, you become a lighthouse for others still sitting in the shadows, waiting for someone brave enough to go first.

"I stand, even when I'm afraid."

K.H.

“Perfection poisons progress. Breathe. Begin again.”

K.H.

CHAPTER 6

Progress Over Perfection

"Done is better than perfect."

SHERYL SANDBERG

Perfection is a liar. It whispers that you'll start when things are just right, when you've learned enough, planned enough, polished enough. But perfection isn't preparation—it's procrastination in a tuxedo.

Progress, on the other hand, is messy. It's crooked lines, awkward first tries, and plenty of do-overs. But progress moves you forward; perfection keeps you frozen.

Harvard psychologists studying goal achievement found that people who focused on progress over perfection were more resilient, less stressed, and ultimately more successful. They called it the "growth mindset effect." Progress keeps you motivated because it builds momentum. Perfection kills motivation because the goal is never good enough.

Yale research on learning shows that mistakes are not setbacks—they're neural upgrades. Each error forces your brain to rewire itself for deeper understanding. Failure is data, not doom.

Think about every great invention, every great book, every great leap in history. None of them came out flawless. They were tested, scrapped, revised, and improved. Progress stacked on progress.

Meanwhile, perfectionists often spend years sitting on their gifts, waiting for flawless conditions. And guess what? Conditions are never flawless. The stars don't align. The timing doesn't come. The perfect draft, the perfect speech, the perfect opportunity—they don't exist.

What exists is today. What exists is the next step. What exists is the courage to move forward, messy and real.

Progress is honest. Perfection is an illusion. Breathe. Begin again.

Because the world doesn't need your perfection. It needs your present.

And the difference between people who talk about dreams and people who live them comes down to one thing: who is willing to make progress without waiting for perfection.

"I choose progress over perfection."

K.H.

"Safety is a necessary illusion. Walk anyway."

K.H.

CHAPTER 7

The Necessary Illusion

"He who is not courageous enough to take risks will accomplish nothing in life."

MUHAMMAD ALI

Safety feels good. Safety feels secure. But let's get real—safety is often just an illusion dressed up in comfort.

You think your job is safe until the company downsizes. You think your relationship is safe until the silence grows louder than the words. You think your routine is safe until the doctor calls with news you weren't ready for.

Life is not safe. It never has been. And waiting for safety before you act is a guaranteed way to stay stuck.

Harvard Business Review has written extensively on risk-taking in leadership, showing that innovation only happens when leaders step beyond the illusion of safety. Playing it safe keeps companies stagnant—and it does the same to people.

Yale studies on human resilience show that people actually thrive under manageable stress. They call it "eustress"—the kind of challenge that stretches you without breaking you. Translation: your growth depends on stepping out of safety.

Most of us cling to the comfort zone like it's home base in a childhood game of tag. Safe, yes. But you don't score points standing still.

Here's the truth: safety is borrowed time. It can vanish in an instant. Which means the real security isn't in avoiding risk—it's in building the strength to walk through it.

Walking anyway means daring to leap even when the net is invisible. It means trusting that you'll grow wings on the way down. It means refusing to let fear chain you to a life smaller than the one you're capable of living.

Safety is an illusion. Courage is real. And walking anyway is how you claim it.

Because the people who change the world are not the ones who waited for guarantees. They are the ones who moved forward.

"I walk forward, even when safety is a myth."

K.H.

“Happiness is being here, not going there. Return to your breath.”

K.H.

CHAPTER 8

Return to Your Breath

"Feelings come and go like clouds in a windy sky. Conscious breathing is my anchor."

THICH NHAT HANH

Breath is the one thing you carry with you from your first moment to your last. It's simple, silent, and always available. And yet most of us treat breathing like background noise—until we're gasping for air in panic, stress, or exhaustion.

Here's the truth: your breath is your built-in reset button.

When life feels overwhelming, when the noise is too loud, when your mind won't shut up—your breath is how you come back. It's the string that ties your body, mind, and spirit together in the present.

Harvard Medical School studies have shown that controlled breathing lowers blood pressure, decreases stress hormones, and activates the parasympathetic nervous system—the body's natural relaxation response. Translation: breathing isn't just spiritual, it's physiological medicine.

Yale researchers have studied the effects of breathwork on students facing high anxiety and found measurable reductions in stress and improved emotional regulation after just weeks of practice. [4] Breathing literally rewires your brain's relationship with stress.

But we forget. We chase happiness in jobs, money, or relationships. The quote reminds us: "Happiness is being here, not going there." You don't have to run across the world to find peace. You can just to return to your breath.

Each inhale is an invitation. Each exhale is a letting go. The more you practice, the more you realize happiness isn't a destination—it's an inhale away.

So the next time your mind races toward tomorrow or drags you back into yesterday, pause. Anchor yourself. Return to your breath. Because in that simple act, you'll find the happiness you've been chasing everywhere else.

Your breath is the pebble you carry that never leaves your pocket. It's always enough. It's always now.

"I return to my breath, and I return to myself."

K.H.

[4] YaleNews, "To Improve Students' Mental Health, Yale Study Finds, Teach Them to Breathe," July 27, 2020, https://news.yale.edu/2020/07/27/improve-students-mental-health-yale-study-finds-teach-them-breathe.

"Listening is love. Let your ears open your heart."

K.H.

CHAPTER 9

Listening Is Love

"Most people do not listen with the intent to understand; they listen with the intent to reply."

STEPHEN R. COVEY

We live in a loud world. Everyone is talking, posting, preaching, and performing. But few people are truly listening. And that's why listening has become a radical act of love.

When you listen, really listen, you're not just hearing words—you're hearing someone's heart. You're creating a sacred space where another person feels seen, valued, and safe.

Harvard research on communication shows that active listening strengthens trust, deepens connection, and improves collaboration. In relationships, listening is often rated as more important than speaking when it comes to long-term satisfaction. Translation: people don't connect with your words—they connect with how you hear them.

Yale studies on empathy found that when people feel listened to, their brain releases oxytocin—the bonding hormone. This means that listening doesn't just feel good emotionally—it literally changes someone's physiology.

But here's the problem: most people listen to respond, not to understand. They're busy planning their reply instead of opening their heart. That's not listening—that's waiting for your turn.

Listening as love means quieting your ego, shutting down your assumptions, and leaning in with presence. It means your ears become an extension of your heart.

There's also value in listening inward. Your body, your emotions, your spirit—they're always speaking. But if you're too distracted, you miss the wisdom they're offering. Listening to yourself is just as vital as listening to others.

Think about it: the people who changed your life probably weren't the loudest. They were the ones who paused, leaned in, and truly heard you. That's listening. That's love.

So in a noisy world, dare to be quiet enough to hear. Because listening is love, and love is what the world needs most.

"I listen with love, and I hear what hearts cannot say aloud."

K.H.

“To heal is to bring the darkness to light. You are the candle.”

K.H.

CHAPTER 10

You Are the Candle

"There is a crack in everything, that's how the light gets in."

LEONARD COHEN

Healing isn't about erasing the dark—it's about bringing light into it. The good news? You already carry the flame.

To heal is to shine even when the shadows feel overwhelming. It's to recognize that your scars aren't signs of weakness but evidence of survival. Every time you light your candle in the dark, you prove that hope is stronger than despair.

Harvard research on trauma recovery shows that healing happens not by forgetting pain, but by reframing it—by finding meaning and building resilience in the aftermath. Survivors who focus on growth, rather than erasure, experience greater well-being and even post-traumatic growth.

Yale studies on resilience echo this: when people see themselves as active participants in their own healing—as the candle, not just the darkness—they recover faster, adapt better, and live fuller lives. Healing is less about what happened to you and more about how you light it up with meaning.

But here's the truth: healing is not a straight line. It's messy. Some days you shine bright. Other days your flame flickers. That's okay. What matters is that you keep relighting.

Don't underestimate the ripple of your light. One candle doesn't just brighten your own space—it sparks the courage for others to light theirs. Your healing becomes a beacon.

So remember this: you are not broken. You are the candle. And every time you bring your darkness into the light, you burn brighter than before.

"I carry the flame of healing within me."

K.H.

"Absence is a powerful presence. Feel the outline of missing."

K.H.

CHAPTER 11

The Outline of Missing

"What we have once enjoyed deeply we can never lose...All that we love deeply becomes a part of us."

HELEN KELLER

Loss leaves a mark. It doesn't vanish with time, but instead reshapes the way we see the world. The empty chair, the quiet room, the memory that sneaks in when you least expect it—absence has a presence all its own.

We're taught to avoid grief, to rush through it, to replace what's missing with busyness. But grief is not something to fix—it's something to feel. Because absence itself becomes a presence, a reminder of what mattered and what shaped us.

Harvard research on grief shows that trying to suppress loss often intensifies suffering. Healthy grieving isn't about erasing absence but integrating it—allowing the outline of what's missing to become part of who we are.

Yale studies on memory reveal that the brain keeps emotional bonds alive even when someone is gone. That's why grief feels like presence—it literally is. Your mind holds onto those connections because love doesn't end when life does.

The outline of a loss is painful, but it's also powerful. It teaches us what truly matters. It deepens our empathy, softens our pride, and reminds us of the fleeting nature of time.

Instead of running from absence, we can lean into it. We can honor it. The silence of loss can become the canvas for gratitude, memory, and meaning.

Grief is not emptiness—it's evidence of love. And feeling its absence doesn't weaken you. It makes you human.

So when you feel the ache of missing, don't hide from it. Trace it. Let it shape you. Because the outline of what's missing is proof that something mattered deeply—and that kind of love is never really gone.

"I honor the presence in what is missing."

K.H.

“Love is allowing the other to become. Release your grip.”

K.H.

CHAPTER 12

Release Your Grip

"If you love someone, set them free. If they come back, they're yours; if they don't, they never were."

RICHARD BACH

Love isn't control. Love isn't ownership. Love isn't chaining someone to your expectations. Real love is freedom—the courage to let another person become fully themselves, even if it scares you.

We often mistake attachment for love. We cling, we demand, we grip tighter when we feel insecure. But gripping isn't loving—it's strangling.

Harvard research on relationships shows that the healthiest bonds are built on autonomy and respect, not control. Couples who allow each other space to grow individually report greater satisfaction and longevity. Why? Because love thrives in freedom, not captivity.

Yale studies on emotional development confirm this: when people feel supported but not smothered, they flourish. They take risks, pursue growth, and build deeper trust with the people who let them breathe.

Releasing your grip doesn't mean you stop caring. It doesn't mean abandonment. It involves trust—trust that love is strong enough to handle freedom. Trust that the bond is deeper than fear.

Think about a tree: if you strangle its roots, it dies. But if you give it space, it grows taller, stronger, more alive. Love works the same way.

Releasing your grip is an act of courage. It's saying, "I choose your becoming over my control." It's believing that real love doesn't shrink—it expands.

So loosen your fists. Open your hands. Let the people you love breathe, stretch, and become. Because love that grips is fear. Love that releases is freedom.

And freedom is where love does its best work.

"I love with open hands, not clenched fists."

K.H.

“Negatives develop in darkness. But so do stars.”

K.H.

CHAPTER 13

Stars in the Dark

"Only in the darkness can you see the stars."

MARTIN LUTHER KING JR.

Darkness has a reputation for being the enemy. We run from it, fear it, curse it. But darkness is also the womb of growth. It's the quiet soil where roots take hold, the night sky where stars reveal their brilliance, the unseen space that forges resilience.

Painful seasons feel like negatives—like the world is printing out a picture you don't want to see. But just as old photographs developed in darkness, your challenges are developing you. The process is uncomfortable, but it's how your true image emerges.

Harvard psychologists studying post-traumatic growth found that people who endured hardship often reported greater strength, deeper appreciation for life, and stronger relationships. Pain reshaped them—not into weaker versions, but into wiser ones.

Yale neuroscience research shows that the brain adapts under pressure, creating new neural pathways when faced with adversity. It means the dark doesn't just test you—it creates you.

Only the backdrop of night reveals a star's shine. Your challenges serve the same purpose—they contrast your strength, courage, and light against the shadow.

So the next time you find yourself in a dark season, don't panic. Look up. Notice the stars. Remember that growth is happening underground, in silence, in the unseen. And trust that when the light returns, you'll rise stronger, clearer, brighter.

Negatives develop in darkness. But so do stars. And so do you.

"Even in darkness,
I am becoming."

K.H.

"Chew carefully. Not all sweetness is truth."

K.H.

CHAPTER 14

Sweet Isn't Always Truth

"Better an honest enemy than a false friend."

GERMAN PROVERB

Sweetness is seductive. We crave words that comfort us, stories that flatter us, and promises that soothe our fear. But sweetness without substance is just sugar—and too much sugar makes you sick.

Truth isn't always sweet. In fact, the truths that save us often taste bitter. They challenge our illusions, disrupt our comfort, and demand our growth. But once digested, they nourish us.

Harvard research on deception found that people often prefer comforting lies to uncomfortable truths, even when lies create long-term harm. Our brains are wired to seek pleasure and avoid pain, so we instinctively lean toward sweetness, even if it poisons us slowly.

Yale studies on cognitive bias confirm this. Humans fall victim to confirmation bias—the tendency to embrace information that feels good and ignore what doesn't. This means we're vulnerable to manipulation, self-deception, and denial, all wrapped in the sugar of half-truths.

But here's the thing: false sweetness rots trust. Once exposed, it leaves scars deeper than the sting of honesty. That's why authentic leaders, lovers, and friends choose honesty over flattery. They chew carefully. They tell the truth, even when it's sharp.

Chewing carefully means asking yourself: Is this sweet because it's nourishing or sweet because it's easy? Does it strengthen me or sedate me? Does it challenge me to grow or lull me to sleep?

So chew carefully. Choose wisely. Because your soul deserves nourishment, not poison wrapped in sugar.

"I choose honesty,
even when it stings."

K.H.

“Overconsumption wastes the soul. Let stillness feed you.”

K.H.

CHAPTER 15

Let Stillness Feed You

"Within you there is a stillness and a sanctuary to which you can retreat at any time."

HERMANN HESSE

We are drowning in consumption. Not just food, but media, noise, opinions, and endless scrolling. We binge on distraction until our souls are bloated and starved at the same time. The more we consume, the emptier we feel.

Here's the truth: overconsumption wastes the soul. Stillness nourishes it.

Stillness is not doing nothing. Stillness is deliberate. It's choosing to pause, to breathe, to listen instead of scroll, to sit instead of sprint. It's the kind of rest that provides nourishment, not numbness.

Harvard research on mindfulness shows that intentional stillness reduces anxiety, improves focus, and boosts emotional well-being. People who practiced even ten minutes of mindful stillness each day reported better decision-making and deeper satisfaction.

Yale studies on digital consumption found that constant exposure to social media overloads the brain's reward system, creating addiction-like patterns that drain energy and self-worth. In contrast, intentional breaks—stillness—reset the brain, restoring clarity and calm.

We live in a culture that glorifies hustle and mocks stillness. But hustle without pause is burnout. Consumption without digestion is sickness. You can't feed your soul if you never stop swallowing.

Stillness is the meal your spirit starves for. It's in stillness that creativity sparks, insight arrives, and peace grows. It's in the pause that you remember who you are beneath the noise.

Overconsumption wastes the soul. Let stillness feed you. Because your best self doesn't come from what you consume—it comes from what you allow to grow in the quiet.

"I feed my soul with stillness, not noise."

K.H.

“Learning is teaching yourself. You are the student and the sage.”

K.H.

CHAPTER 16

Student and Sage

"Education is the kindling of a flame, not the filling of a vessel."

SOCRATES

We've been taught to see learning as something that happens in classrooms, through degrees, with someone older or wiser at the front of the room. But real learning is a self-driven fire. And here's the twist—you're both the student and the sage.

Every time you seek knowledge, you're the student. Every time you apply it, teach it, or live it, you're the sage. Growth isn't about waiting for someone to hand you wisdom—it's about discovering the wisdom within.

Harvard research on self-directed learning shows that people retain more knowledge when they pursue it voluntarily, rather than being forced. Ownership transforms learning from obligation into empowerment.

Yale neuroscience studies reveal that teaching others strengthens your own neural connections, making you remember and understand the material more deeply. The best way to master something is to become both the learner and the teacher.

But too often, we trap ourselves in self-doubt. We think, "I'm not wise enough to lead. I'm not skilled enough to share." Yet the truth is, wisdom grows as you practice it. You don't become the sage after years of perfection—you become the sage by daring to share what you know now.

Being both student and sage means embracing humility and confidence at the same time. It's admitting you don't know it all, while also owning the fact that what you do know has value.

So read, ask, explore, fail, and learn. Then turn around and share, teach, encourage, and lead. Because your voice matters. Your lessons matter. And the cycle of wisdom keeps turning only when you step into both roles.

You are not just absorbing life. You are shaping it. You are not just learning from the world—you are teaching it how to grow through you.

Learning is teaching yourself.

"I learn boldly, and I teach freely."

K.H.

"I may be trustworthy. Even if you don't see it yet."

K.H.

CHAPTER 17

Even If You Don't See It Yet

"Faith is taking the first step even when you don't see the whole staircase."

MARTIN LUTHER KING JR.

Trust is fragile. It's not built in a moment, but in a thousand quiet actions, repeated over time. And often, it's not seen immediately—it's earned in shadows before it's recognized in the light.

Being trustworthy doesn't always mean people will see it right away. Sometimes your integrity is invisible until life tests it. Sometimes your consistency is overlooked until the moment it's needed most.

Harvard research on leadership found that trustworthiness was rated the single most important quality of effective leaders. But it wasn't charisma or brilliance that built trust—it was reliability. Showing up. Keeping promises. Doing what you said you would do.

Yale studies on perception confirm that humans are slow to grant trust but quick to withdraw it when betrayed. That means building trust is a long game—one built on patience, not shortcuts.

You may be trustworthy long before others recognize it. You may walk with integrity long before the world gives you credit. But trust isn't about recognition—it's about alignment. Trust is about being who you say you are, even when nobody is clapping.

And here's the thing: trust also applies inward. You must learn to trust yourself. Your decisions, your instincts, your wisdom. Self-trust is the foundation of confidence, and without it, external trust will always ring hollow.

So keep showing up. Keep your promises. Keep walking in integrity—even if it takes time for others to see it. Trust is about your commitment.

You may be trustworthy. Even if they don't see it yet. And one day, when the test comes, your consistency will speak louder than words.

"I live in integrity, whether or not it's noticed."

K.H.

“Make memories, not just moments. Let life linger.”

K.H.

CHAPTER 18

Let Life Linger

"Enjoy the little things in life, for one day you may look back and realize they were the big things."

ROBERT BRAULT

We rush through life like it's a checklist. Finish school. Get the job. Buy the house. But in our rush to collect milestones, we forget to let moments linger long enough to become memories.

Memories aren't just built by time—they're built by attention. A moment becomes a memory when you slow down enough to feel it, to taste it, to breathe it in fully.

Harvard research on happiness found that the most joyful people weren't the richest or the busiest—they were the ones who practiced savoring. They allowed experiences to stretch longer by being fully present in them.

Yale studies on memory reveal that emotional intensity imprints experiences deeper into the brain. When you savor—when you let life linger—you create stronger, more lasting memories that carry meaning long after the moment ends.

But here's the problem: most of us are sprinting through our days, too distracted to notice the small joys. We consume experiences like fast food—quick, easy, and then forgotten. Slowing down feels countercultural in a world that worships speed.

Yet letting life linger is wisdom. It's understanding that what makes life rich isn't how much you collect, but how deeply you experience it.

Make memories, not just moments. Sit longer at the table with people you love. Watch the sunset until it disappears, not until your phone buzzes. Laugh until your stomach hurts. Write it down. Take a picture. But more importantly—feel it.

Because when the rush of achievement fades, it's the memories—the lingering—that hold you together.

Let life linger. Because what you'll hold onto isn't the timeline. It's the time*less*.

"I slow down to let life linger."

K.H.

"Award yourself the gold stars. You've earned them."

K.H.

CHAPTER 19

Award Yourself

"Celebrate what you've accomplished,
but raise the bar a little higher each time
you succeed."

MIA HAMM

We wait too long for permission to celebrate ourselves. We grind, we hustle, we achieve, and then we shrug it off because it doesn't feel "big enough" yet. We hand out applause to others but forget to clap for the person staring back in the mirror.

Here's the truth: you don't need the world's approval to validate your effort. You don't need someone else to hang a medal around your neck. You are allowed to award yourself.

Harvard research on motivation found that celebrating small wins creates momentum. When you acknowledge progress, your brain releases dopamine—the chemical of motivation and reward. This isn't just feel-good fluff; it's biology fueling your drive forward.

Yale studies on self-compassion show that people who recognize their own efforts are more resilient, less prone to burnout, and more likely to reach long-term goals. Beating yourself up doesn't build success—encouragement does.

But most of us have been taught that self-praise is arrogance. We confuse confidence with conceit, humility with self-erasure. The truth is, humility isn't pretending you're not good enough—it's knowing your worth without needing to shout it.

Awarding yourself a gold star isn't about bragging—it's about balance. It's about giving your brain the fuel it needs to keep climbing.

So write down your wins. Toast to your effort. Stand in the mirror and say, "Well done." Because progress deserves a party, no matter how small the step.

Award yourself. You've earned it. And the more you honor your effort, the more fuel you'll have to keep going.

"I celebrate myself without apology."

K.H.

“Stay or cross but don’t camp in the shadows.”

K.H.

CHAPTER 20

Don't Camp in the Shadows

"In the middle of every difficulty lies opportunity."

ALBERT EINSTEIN

Life will hand you shadows—seasons of uncertainty, struggle, and pain. You can't always choose whether you'll walk through them, but you can choose how long you stay.

Some people make a home in the shadows. They pitch tents in bitterness, build walls out of fear, and convince themselves the darkness is safer than risking the light. But shadows aren't meant to be permanent addresses. They're rest stops, not destinations.

Harvard research on resilience shows that people who frame challenges as temporary setbacks recover faster and bounce back stronger. When you believe the shadow is forever, you surrender. When you believe it's temporary, you endure.

Yale studies on stress adaptation reveal that the human brain is incredibly malleable—able to grow, adapt, and rewire itself in response to hardship. This means your time in the shadows can build strength if you keep moving, instead of camping there.

Shadows test you, but they also teach you. They remind you of the light you crave, the purpose you carry, and the resilience you didn't know you had. But only if you keep walking.

Staying stuck—camping in the shadows—turns temporary trials into lifelong prisons. The longer you stay, the more comfortable the darkness feels, until you forget what light looks like.

So yes, pause if you must. Rest if you need. But don't build your life in the shadows. Cross through. Step out. Keep moving.

Because the light is always waiting—but only for those who refuse to camp in the dark.

"I walk through shadows, but I do not live there."

K.H.

"You are your enthusiasms. Fan your flame."

K.H.

CHAPTER 21

Fan Your Flame

"A candle loses nothing by lighting another candle."

JAMES KELLER

Enthusiasm is fuel. It's the spark that ignites your creativity, the energy that pulls others into your orbit, and the passion that keeps you moving when discipline feels heavy. You are your enthusiasms—what excites you, drives you, and lights you up is not just a hobby; it's your fire.

But flames die if they're not fed. Ignore your passions long enough, and your life becomes a slow burn of obligation. Numb, dull, and quietly suffocating.

Harvard research on workplace fulfillment found that people who engage in passion-driven work report higher resilience, creativity, and well-being. Passion doesn't just make you feel good—it makes you stronger.

Yale studies on motivation reveal that intrinsic enthusiasm—doing something because it lights you up inside—creates longer-lasting drive than external rewards like money or status. Translation: the flame that burns brightest is the one you fan from within.

But the world is full of buckets of water: critics, cynics, fear, and distraction. If you're not careful, you'll let others smother your flame before it ever gets a chance to shine. Protecting your fire isn't selfish—it's essential.

Fanning your flame means chasing what energizes you, not what drains you. It means saying *yes* to what sparks joy and *no* to what douses your spirit. It means surrounding yourself with people who pour oxygen, not water, on your dreams.

And here's the best part: your flame doesn't diminish when you share it. Enthusiasm is contagious. The more you fan your flame, the more others around you remember their own.

So guard it. Feed it. Protect it. Fan your flame—because the world needs your fire, and so do you.

"I feed my fire, and
I let it shine."

K.H.

"Be at the center. But not the center of everything."

K.H.

CHAPTER 22

Not the Center of Everything

"Humility is not thinking less of yourself, it's thinking of yourself less."

RICK WARREN[5]

There's a fine line between confidence and self-absorption. Standing at the center of your life is powerful. Believing the world revolves around you? That's a trap.

You should be at the center—responsible for your choices, aware of your power, committed to your growth. But the second you confuse being the center of your life with being the center of everyone else's, you lose perspective and connection.

Harvard research on leadership shows that humility is one of the strongest predictors of long-term success. Leaders who balance confidence with humility create stronger teams, deeper loyalty, and more sustainable results.

Yale studies on empathy reveal that people who maintain perspective-taking—seeing beyond themselves—experience greater

[5] Rick Warren, *The Purpose Driven Life: What on Earth Am I Here For?* (Grand Rapids, MI: Zondervan, 2002), 149.

emotional intelligence and healthier relationships. Translation: balance your center with theirs.

Being at the center means owning your worth, not inflating it. It means knowing you matter deeply, but so does everyone else. It's confidence with roots, not ego with claws.

And here's the paradox: when you stop trying to be the center of everything, your influence grows. Because people trust those who see beyond themselves.

So be bold. Be central in your own life. But don't confuse that with being the sun in everyone else's life. You are a star, yes—but one among many, part of a greater constellation.

Be at the center. But not the center of everything. That's how you shine without burning others out.

*"I stand at my center,
with humility and grace."*

K.H.

“Only outliers tell the truth. Be brave enough to stand outside.”

K.H.

CHAPTER 23

Brave Enough to Stand Outside

"The reward for conformity is that everyone likes you but yourself."

RITA MAE BROWN

The crowd feels safe. Inside the circle, you blend in, avoid judgment, and stay wrapped in the comfort of belonging. But here's the truth: crowds rarely change the world. Outliers do.

Standing outside is uncomfortable. It means risking criticism, rejection, and misunderstanding. It means being seen as strange before being recognized as visionary. But every truth-teller, innovator, and trailblazer had to leave the crowd to find their voice.

Harvard research on innovation shows that nonconformists are the ones who drive progress. They're willing to challenge assumptions, question norms, and risk failure to find better ways forward. Without outliers, we'd still be stuck repeating the same patterns, mistaking tradition for truth.

Yale psychology studies confirm that social pressure is one of the strongest forces shaping human behavior. Most people conform, even when they know the group is wrong, simply to avoid standing out. Conformity feels safe, but it silences truth.

Being brave enough to stand outside doesn't mean rejecting community. It means refusing to trade your integrity for approval. It means choosing truth over comfort, growth over acceptance.

Yes, standing outside can be lonely. But it also gives you a perspective the crowd can't see. From the edge, you notice what others overlook. From the outside, you can speak what others are afraid to admit.

So if the choice is between betraying yourself to fit in or standing outside to live in truth—choose the outside. Because the world doesn't need more echoes. It needs voices brave enough to be original.

Only outliers tell the truth. Be brave enough to stand outside.

"I choose truth over conformity, even if I stand alone."

K.H.

“Love and hate twist. Untangle with care.”

K.H.

CHAPTER 24

Untangle with Care

"There is no remedy for love but to love more."

HENRY DAVID THOREAU

Love and hate often live closer than we like to admit. Both are passionate, consuming, and deeply tied to what we value most. That's why when relationships break, when trust is betrayed, or when expectations collapse, love can twist into hate—and back again.

The tangle of emotions is messy. One moment you're full of tenderness, the next you're fueled by resentment. This is the paradox of intimacy: the people who can bring you the most joy can also bring you the most pain.

Harvard research on emotional regulation shows that suppressing these conflicting feelings only intensifies them. Avoidance makes the knot tighter. Facing the tangle—naming it, feeling it, working through it—loosens the grip.

Yale psychologists studying forgiveness found that people who process hurt with empathy and honesty, instead of revenge or suppression, experience lower stress, stronger immune systems, and healthier relationships. Untangling doesn't mean excusing harm—it means choosing not to stay trapped in it.

Untangling with care requires patience. It means resisting the urge to rip through the knot just to make it disappear. It means sitting with your feelings long enough to separate love from hurt, anger from longing, truth from illusion.

How you untangle emotions shapes what comes next. Pull too hard, and you risk breaking the thread entirely. Move gently, and you preserve space for healing, reconciliation, or at least peace within yourself.

Love and hate knot. That's human. But your response is where power lives. You can choose to stay tangled, or you can untangle with care.

Because in the end, the goal isn't to erase the knot—it's to free yourself from its chokehold and move forward lighter, wiser, stronger.

"I untangle my emotions with patience and care."

K.H.

“I win, you win. The only way that matters.”

K.H.

CHAPTER 25

The Only Win That Matters

"If you want to go fast, go alone. If you want to go far, go together."

AFRICAN PROVERB

We live in a culture obsessed with competition. From classrooms to boardrooms, from playgrounds to politics, we're taught to measure success by how many people we've outperformed. But the victories that matter most aren't about leaving others behind—they're about lifting others up with you.

Success doesn't have to be a zero-sum game. Real winning is shared. When your growth helps others grow, when your light sparks someone else's fire, when your win opens doors for those around you—that's the win that matters.

Harvard Business Review studies on leadership and collaboration show that teams rooted in cooperation consistently outperform those fueled by rivalry. Shared success builds trust, creativity, and resilience. In contrast, toxic competition breeds burnout, fear, and isolation.

Yale research on human motivation reveals that people experience deeper satisfaction when they contribute to collective goals rather than just personal gain. Helping others thrive activates the brain's reward circuits more powerfully than selfish achievement. It means we're wired to win *together*.

But culture often tells us otherwise. We're told that for someone to win, someone else must lose. That lie keeps us small, suspicious, and disconnected.

Imagine instead a mindset of abundance: "I win; you win." It doesn't mean there won't be challenges. It means your success doesn't threaten mine, and mine doesn't diminish yours. It means there's room at the table for everyone, and the table gets bigger the more we share.

The only win that matters is collective. Because at the end of your life, it won't be the trophies or titles that last—it'll be the lives you touched.

"I rise higher by helping others rise with me."

K.H.

“Kindness is not weakness. Choose the softer space.”

K.H.

CHAPTER 26

Choose the Softer Space

"In a gentle way, you can shake the world."

MAHATMA GANDHI

Strength is often mistaken for hardness—sharp words, clenched fists, unyielding stances. But real strength often shows up in softness. It's the courage to stay gentle in a harsh world, the wisdom to respond with compassion when anger is easier.

Choosing the softer space doesn't mean avoiding conflict or pretending all is fine. It means meeting life with empathy instead of ego, with patience instead of pride.

Harvard research on emotional intelligence shows that leaders who practice kindness and empathy create healthier, more productive environments than those who lead with fear. Kindness is a powerful skill.

Yale studies on compassion demonstrate that acts of gentleness trigger oxytocin release in both giver and receiver, strengthening bonds and reducing stress. The science is clear: kindness heals not just relationships, but bodies and minds.

Yes, softness feels risky. The world tells us that to survive, we must armor up, toughen up, and never let our guard down. Yet the very armor that protects us also isolates us.

Softness, on the other hand, connects us. It allows intimacy, trust, and love to flow. It makes space for forgiveness, understanding, and growth.

Choosing the softer space is not a weakness—it's a radical strength. It's the decision to disarm in a world obsessed with weapons. It's the choice to be water instead of stone, knowing water can carve through mountains.

So the next time you're tempted to harden, pause. Ask yourself: What would softness do here? And then choose it—not because it's easy, but because it's powerful.

"I choose kindness, even when it feels risky."

K.H.

"Don't rush your becoming. Your becoming is beautiful."

K.H.

CHAPTER 27

Your Becoming Is Beautiful

"And the day came when the risk to remain tight in a bud was more painful than the risk it took to blossom."

ANAÏS NIN

Becoming is not a single moment—it's a lifelong unfolding. Too often, we treat growth like a finish line: once we arrive, then we'll finally be enough. But the truth is, you are already in the process of becoming, and that process itself is beautiful.

Growth is messy. It's full of false starts, detours, and seasons where nothing seems to bloom. But even in those quiet stretches, change is happening underground. Just as seeds crack in darkness before they rise into the light, your becoming often takes root where no one else can see.

Harvard psychologists studying human development emphasize that identity is fluid—constantly evolving through experience. The self isn't fixed, but flexible. Every challenge, every heartbreak, every victory shapes who you are becoming.

Yale research on resilience highlights that people who embrace the process of becoming—rather than rushing to outcomes—

experience deeper fulfillment and stronger mental health. Trusting the process is itself an act of courage.

But many of us get stuck when we compare our becoming to someone else's. We scroll, we measure, we envy. And in doing so, we forget that becoming is not a race. It's a deeply personal unfolding that cannot be timed against another's.

Your becoming is beautiful precisely because it's yours. No one else has walked your exact path, carried your exact scars, or held your exact hopes. Your becoming is not late, not lacking, not less—it's perfect in its timing.

Don't rush your becoming. Don't shame it. Don't compare it. Instead, honor it. Celebrate the ways you're unfolding right now, even if the blossom isn't fully open yet.

Because one day, you'll look back and realize: the beauty wasn't only in the bloom—it was in every step of the becoming.

"I honor my becoming—
it is beautiful."

K.H.

ABOUT THE AUTHOR

Kelvin Harris is a writer and motivator from New Haven, Connecticut. His passion is helping others unlock their inner strength through words that inspire action.

Pebbles in My Pocket is his debut collection of motivational affirmations, written to fuel resilience and hope.

BIBLIOGRAPHY

African Proverb. "If you want to go fast, go alone; if you want to go far, go together." Commonly attributed proverb; primary source unknown.

Ali, Muhammad, with Richard Durham. *The Greatest: My Own Story*. New York: Random House, 1975.

Amabile, Teresa M., and Steven J. Kramer. "The Power of Small Wins." *Harvard Business Review* 89, no. 5 (May 2011). https://hbr.org/2011/05/the-power-of-small-wins.

Bach, Richard. *Illusions: The Adventures of a Reluctant Messiah*. New York: Dell, 1977.

Benson, Herbert. *The Relaxation Response*. New York: William Morrow, 1975.

Brault, Robert. Quotation originally printed in *National Enquirer*, 1985; reprinted in *Reader's Digest*, "Quotable Quotes," September 1986, p. 139: "Enjoy the little things in life, for one day you may look back and realize they were the big things."

Brown, Rita Mae. *Venus Envy*. New York: Bantam, 1993.

Cohen, Leonard. "Anthem." Track on *The Future*. Columbia Records, 1992.

Covey, Stephen R. *The 7 Habits of Highly Effective People*. New York: Free Press, 1989.

Einstein, Albert. "In the middle of every difficulty lies opportunity." Commonly attributed quotation; no definitive primary source identified. See Quote Investigator. "In the Middle of Difficulty Lies Opportunity." Last modified March 10, 2013. https://quoteinvestigator.com/2013/03/10/in-the-middle-of-difficulty-lies-opportunity/.

Elliot, Jim. *The Journals of Jim Elliot*. Grand Rapids, MI: Revell, 1978.

Gandhi, Mohandas K. "In a gentle way, you can shake the world." Attributed; no definitive primary source identified.

Gandhi, Mohandas K. "The future depends on what you do today." Attributed; no definitive primary source identified.

German Proverb. "Better an honest enemy than a false friend."

Hamm, Mia. *Go for the Goal: A Champion's Guide to Winning in Soccer and Life*. New York: HarperCollins, 1999.

Harvard Health Publishing. "Relaxation techniques: Breath control helps quell errant stress response." July 24, 2024. https://www.health.harvard.edu/mind-and-mood/relaxation-techniques-breath-control-helps-quell-errant-stress-response/.

Hemingway, Ernest. "Courage is grace under pressure." Commonly attributed aphorism; see multiple attributions in interviews/essays.

Hesse, Hermann. *Siddhartha: An Indian Tale.* Translated by Hilda Rosner. New York: New Directions, 1951.

Holy Bible, English Standard Version. Wheaton, IL: Crossway, 2001.

Keller, Helen. "What we have once enjoyed deeply we can never lose...All that we love deeply becomes a part of us." In *We Bereaved* (1929) [letter; attribution common].

Keller, James. *You Can Change the World*. New York: P. J. Kenedy & Sons, 1948.

Killingsworth, Matthew A., and Daniel T. Gilbert. "A Wandering Mind Is an Unhappy Mind." *Science* 330, no. 6006 (2010): 932. https://doi.org/10.1126/science.1192439.

King, Martin Luther, Jr. *Strength to Love*. New York: Harper & Row, 1963.

Nhat Hanh, Thich. *The Miracle of Mindfulness: An Introduction to the Practice of Meditation*. Boston: Beacon Press, 1975.

Nin, Anaïs. *The Diary of Anaïs Nin, Volume IV: 1944–1947.* Edited by Gunther Stuhlmann. New York: Harcourt Brace Jovanovich, 1971.

Ophir, Eyal, Clifford Nass, and Anthony D. Wagner. "Cognitive Control in Media Multitaskers." *Proceedings of the National Academy of Sciences* 106, no. 37 (2009): 15583–87. https://doi.org/10.1073/pnas.0903620106.

Plutarch. *"On Listening."* In *Moralia.* Translated by Robin Waterfield. Oxford: Oxford University Press, 1992.

Quote Investigator. "Education Is Not the Filling of a Pail, but the Lighting of a Fire." Last modified March 28, 2013. https://quoteinvestigator.com/2013/03/28/mind-fire/.

Ram Dass. *Be Here Now*. San Cristobal, NM: Lama Foundation, 1971.

Sandberg, Sheryl. *Lean In: Women, Work, and the Will to Lead*. New York: Alfred A. Knopf, 2013.

Seppälä, Emma M., Christina M. Bradley, Judith T. Moskowitz, Marcela C. Ospina, and Laurie R. Santos. "Promoting Mental Health and Psychological Thriving in University Students: A Randomized Controlled Trial of Three Well-Being Interventions." *Frontiers in Psychiatry* 11 (2020): 590. https://doi.org/10.3389/fpsyt.2020.00590.

Thoreau, Henry David. *The Writings of Henry D. Thoreau: Journal, Volume 9, 1851–1854*. Edited by Bradford Torrey and Francis H. Allen. Boston: Houghton Mifflin, 1906.

Warren, Rick. *The Purpose Driven Life: What on Earth Am I Here For?* Grand Rapids, MI: Zondervan, 2002.

YaleNews. "To Improve Students' Mental Health, Yale Study Finds, Teach Them to Breathe." July 27, 2020. https://news.yale.edu/2020/07/27/improve-students-mental-health-yale-study-finds-teach-them-breathe.

www.ingramcontent.com/pod-product-compliance
Lightning Source LLC
Chambersburg PA
CBHW070642130626
46555CB00006B/2657

9798994055304